M000086125

A Birthday Surprise

by Jack Conway
illustrated by Naomi Lewis

SCHOOL PUBLISHERS

Printed in Mexico

ISBN 10: 0-15-349986-9
ISBN 13: 978-0-15-349986-9

Ordering Options
ISBN 10: 0-15-349937-0 (Grade 2 ELL Collection)
ISBN 13: 978-0-15-349937-1 (Grade 2 ELL Collection)
ISBN 10: 0-15-357225-6 (package of 5)
ISBN 13: 978-0-15-357225-8 (package of 5)

1 2 3 4 5 6 7 8 9 10   050   15 14 13 12 11 10 09 08 07 06

Characters

Narrator

Mom

Dad

Juan

Maria

Setting: A room filled with
decorations for a birthday party

4

Narrator: Juan's family has moved to a new house. It is Juan's birthday. He is seven years old.

Maria: Happy birthday, Juan!

Juan: Thank you!

6

Mom: Here is a present from Dad, Maria, and me.

Dad: Happy birthday, Juan! You can open your present now.

Narrator: Juan opens his present.

Juan: Wow! It's a soccer ball. I wanted a new soccer ball. Thank you!

Maria: We will all enjoy your birthday party this afternoon, Juan.

Juan: I wish my friends from our old neighborhood were coming.

Mom: I'm sure you will have fun with your new friends, Juan.

Juan: I know I will!

Dad: There is still one more birthday surprise to come, Juan.

Narrator: Mom, Dad, and Maria smile at each other.

Juan: What is it? I can't wait!

Narrator: The children arrive for Juan's party that afternoon.

Mom: Your guests are here!

Maria: Your friends from your new school are here, Juan.

12

Dad: We asked some of your friends from our old neighborhood, too!

Narrator: Juan's friends from his old neighborhood shout, "Surprise!"

Juan: Thank you! This is a nice birthday surprise.

Narrator: Juan has a very happy birthday with all his friends together.

14

Scaffolded Language Development

OPPOSITES Review describing words with children. Write the following describing words on the board: *old* and *new*. Explain that these words mean the opposite of each other. Model opposites using the following examples: *This book is old. This book is new.* If possible, hold up an old book and a new book when you read the sentences. Then have students read the sentences below, and choose the word from the word bank that means the opposite of the underlined word in each sentence. Have students chorally read each sentence with the opposite word instead of the underlined word.

Word Bank: quiet, big, short, light

1. The <u>heavy</u> box is over there.
2. The <u>little</u> kitten is playing.
3. The dog has a <u>loud</u> bark.
4. The kite has a <u>long</u> tail.

🍁 Science

Write Sentences Juan's family gave him a soccer ball for his birthday. Guide children in writing sentences that tell about what would happen to the ball if Juan was holding the ball and let go of it. Make sure children give reasons for their answers.

School-Home Connection

Birthday Surprise Ask children to talk about the book with family members. Then talk about whether they would like to have a surprise birthday party.

Word Count: 215